Why Investing in Dividend Stocks Makes Sense.

By D.K. Hawkins

Series "Personal Finance for You"

Why Investing in Dividend Stocks Makes Sense

Series "Personal Finance for You"
By: D.K. Hawkins
Version 1.1 ~May 2021
Published by D.K. Hawkins at KDP
Copyright ©2021 by D.K. Hawkins. All rights reserved.

No part of this publication may be reproduced, distributed or transmitted in any form or by any means including photocopying, recording or other electronic or mechanical methods or by any information storage or retrieval system without the prior written permission of the publishers, except in the case of very brief quotations embodied in critical reviews and certain other noncommercial uses permitted by copyright law.

All rights reserved, including the right of reproduction in whole or in part in any form.

All information in this book has been carefully researched and checked for factual accuracy. However, the author and publisher make no warranty, express or implied, that the information contained herein is appropriate for every individual, situation, or purpose and assume no responsibility for errors or omissions.

The reader assumes the risk and full responsibility for all actions. The author will not be held responsible for any loss or damage, whether consequential, incidental, special, or otherwise, that may result from the information presented in this book.

All images are free for use or purchased from stock photo sites or royalty-free for commercial use. I have relied on my own observations as well as many different sources for this book, and I have done my best to check facts and give credit where it is due. In the event that any material is used without proper permission, please contact me so that the oversight can be corrected.

The information provided in this book is for informational purposes only and is not intended to be a source of advice or credit analysis with respect to the material presented. The information and/or documents contained in this book do not constitute legal or financial advice and should never be used without first consulting with a financial professional to determine what may be best for your individual needs.

The publisher and the author do not make any guarantee or other promise as to any results that may be obtained from using the content of this book. You should never make any investment decision without first consulting with your own financial advisor and conducting your own research and due diligence. To the maximum extent permitted by law, the publisher and the author disclaim any and all liability in the event any information, commentary, analysis, opinions, advice and/or recommendations contained in this book prove to be inaccurate, incomplete or unreliable, or result in any investment or other losses.

Content contained or made available through this book is not intended to and does not constitute legal advice or investment advice and no attorney-client relationship is formed. The publisher and the author are providing this book and its contents on an "as is" basis. Your use of the information in this book is at your own risk.

Table of Contents

- INTRODUCTION. 5
- CHAPTER ONE 6
  - Investing in Dividend Stocks. 6
  - Why Dividend Stocks Make Great Investments. 11
  - Dividend Investing Strategy 14
  - Criteria to Look For When You Invest In Dividend Stocks. 19
- CHAPTER TWO. 31
  - Dividend Stocks. 31
  - Why dividends matter? 50
  - Why Is Dividend Investing So Popular? 55
  - Best Dividend Stocks to Buy. 64
  - Dividend Stocks and How to Invest in Them. 72
- CHAPTER THREE. 81
  - How Can You Lose Money Investing in Dividend Stocks? 81
  - Stocks That Pay Dividends – Reasons Dividend Stocks May Be Right for You. 85
  - Ways to Find the Best Dividend Stocks. 91
  - Dividend Versus Growth Investments. 94
  - Reasons to Be a Dividend Growth Investor. 97
- CONCLUSION. 107

INTRODUCTION.

Dividend investment can be an excellent strategy for increasing your stock market earnings. There are many reasons, but here is a couple.

The Income: The first excellent thing about stocks of dividends is, of course, their revenue. You can buy a means to a significant income using these shares if you have adequate money. It is also easier to invest in something that gives you a monthly income than to invest in something worthwhile, but you don't notice the money.

Safety: Dividend stocks are several times safer to keep than other investments. Simply because a corporation pays a dividend, it will receive a bonus in the security area for two reasons. First, it'll pay for itself eventually. For example, when a company offers a 5% dividend, it will pay itself in 20 years. Secondly, people flock to these stocks. Whenever an emergency occurs, people try to pull out of dangerous plays to "play safely," which leads to the dividend stocks being generally more effective than any other market in the event of a catastrophe.

Appreciation: The only advantage of holding these shares are not dividends. You can also gain from the value of the stock and the dividends, a type of way to eat and get your cake if you purchase into a substantial stock.

CHAPTER ONE
Investing in Dividend Stocks.

The stock market has been so volatile over the past few years. People who invested in several firms and mutual funds have seen their worth in their portfolios decrease dramatically. While those that stood on the market finally gained most of their money, many eventually lost a significant chunk of their nest egg. Investing in dividend stock could be an excellent alternative for people seeking to invest in future growth and obtain extra cash flow every month. An investor delivers diverse advantages to an investor by investing in dividend stocks.

One of the key advantages of investing in dividend stocks is that they offer an investor a monthly supplementary cash flow. Dividend inventories are stocks of an enterprise that pays its owners a dividend. Typically, payments are provided quarterly or annually based on the company's success in the preceding fiscal year. These distributions generally amount to a few percent, providing a good instant return on investment to the investor. Investors typically choose to receive either a cash payout or other shares instead of a cash payout.

Another advantage of dividend share is that investors also often experience an increase in stock value. The majority of corporations with a long history of payment are pretty powerful enterprises. As these strong organizations often have good financial performance and are efficiently managed, their value of stock shares will likewise improve with time. This could give an investor an even higher return on their investment in dividend shares.

While split stocks could be a terrific strategy to get a solid and stable return on investments, most people must pick carefully to invest in stocks. There is a range of elements to consider when deciding between the various dividend stocks. The stability of dividend payments is one of the essential aspects. You will want to ensure that the corporation always pays dividend shares because of the additional cash flow you would receive. In general, you would like to see the company pay a stable dividend in the last few years.

You will also want to contribute to the strength of the underlying company in addition to looking at the history of dividend payments. Therefore, when you check them, you need to study the firm where you invest and the exact characteristics you want to invest in any other firm. This would involve revising the company's recent financial statements, an appraisal of its position in the industry, and any other factors that might affect its future financial achievements and stock value.

Benefits of Dividend Investing.

1. Get Paid to Wait.

Dividends allow a "waiting payment" for an investor. In history, 43 percent of the S&P 500 total return was delivered by dividends. Thus, dividends offer a continuous return while waiting for an appreciation of capital.

2. Dividend Growth Compounding.

Increasing payouts multiply the benefits of exponential growth. This has to do with increasing the number of shares (reinvestment) and the dividends per share. The exponential potential of compounding dividend growth can deliver competitive returns, whether the stock price improves or not.

3. Taking Advantage of Corrections and Bear Markets.

Investors who are knowledgeable enough to reinvest dividends during corrections and buy more dividend shares when prices are lower will come out ahead in the end. Later, the return is increased by the interim decline in the stock price when prices rebound. Thus, reinvestment of dividends and accumulation of additional shares in adverse markets and corrections considerably improve dividend growth and long-term return on investment.

4. Capital Preservation.

Paying companies with high-quality dividends are more mature and stable than the norm. In general, stocks are higher than speculation stocks in down-market environments. This is especially true when selecting stocks that use a value strategy with a security margin.

Regional blog readers know that the notion of portfolio risk management has been put to the highest importance. Recall that permanent principal loss is the most significant danger of investing.

5. Create an Income Stream.

Dividends provide an ongoing stream of revenue. Although most stocks pay a quarterly dividend, a well-built dividend portfolio can deliver a constant monthly revenue stream. The only way to focus on yield is a big mistake. You want to purchase businesses that can support (and perhaps increase) their dividends.

6. Inflation Hedge.

Fixed income investments have the major disadvantage of not expanding their revenue stream. In just 24 years, even a 3% inflation rate will eliminate 50% of your principal's purchasing power. Dividend stocks give you the ability to earn income which improves and sustains your capital and income's buying power.

Why Dividend Stocks Make Great Investments.

A corporation's primary goal is to pay its shareholders dividends." It was commonly thought that there were speculative gains in stock prices, so the primary reason behind having stocks was to participate in a constant dividend flow.

Many investors had virtually no dividend interest. In the course of that long bull, the enormous increase in stock prices reduced the contribution of dividends to overall gains. No one would seriously suggest that dividends were the principal objective of owning shares.

As we all know, the bull became a bubble, and the bubble exploded from 2000 to 2002 over the next three years. Many people's pension plans had been ruined when the dam came over, and numerous investors sobered up.

The appreciation of dividends and dividend-paying shares has been renewed since 2002. Investors are aware of the possibility that a stock dividend portfolio might reduce risk, increase principal and raise income consistently over time.

You can genuinely have growth and income with solid dividend-paying investments. Splits are the secret weapon of stocks. Studies reveal that nearly half or more of the share market's overall gain has been accountable for dividends over a very long period.

You may be surprised by the modest dividends in advertising. The Dow, S & P 500, and the NASDAQ indices are not extensively published and receive the attention they give each day.

However, all these indices merely reflect changes in prices. As a result, the "how stocks do" is relatively incomplete. It is unusual that so many investors are subject to dividends.

Common misperceptions of dividend stocks are--
- Slow-growing and very boring.
  An indication that companies cannot think of anything better to do with the money, and
- Suitable only for retirees needing income.

All these concepts are wrong. Indeed, dividend-paying equities are attractive for everyone of any age as a fundamental investment.

In fact, the best investment that someone may possess is dividend stocks. Seven explanations for this:

1. A good total return on dividend stocks. Note that overall return is the ultimate objective, not just price assessment. Total return Equals value for money Plus dividends.
2. Dividends are lightly taxed. The Federal dividend tax rate currently exceeds 15%.

3. Dividend practices tend to persist. Solid and long-established dividend-paid corporations are generally. The best of them rarely reduce and grow their dividends. Dividend increases often occur at a much faster rate than many people ever have. (Looking at #5 below.)
4. You don't need to sell the stock. You're just being sent to get the dividend. You can do anything with it: re-invest, save or spend. (See the following #7)
5. Dividend rates may increase with time, as opposed to bonds. And that is precisely what the best dividend stocks do. Over the last three years, the stocks in the S&P 500 have averaged 17% of their dividends each year. No bond will, nor will your local bank. No bond.
6. Also, in contrast to bonds, your principal can increase in time if invested in stocks. This is because bonds are "fixed" investments: you get back your original investment at the end of the bond period... in dollars that are inflation ravaged. On the other hand, stocks have historically been the sole asset type beyond inflation.
7. With your dividends, you can do whatever you please. This money is not 'caught up in the stock's ownership. If you are young, you may want investiture in them to expand your wealth quicker, perhaps in the same firm. This brings into action the "wonder of composition." You can spend the funds on a monthly income if you are retired. Or anybody can do anything between them: re-invest, spend, etc.

8. It's thrilling, rewarding, and fun to own dividend stocks. Most investors would be wise to have a large share of their dividend-paid investments at any age or stage of life.

Dividend Investing Strategy.

1. Embrace an Investing Strategy.

How are you, investors? Value, contrary, growth at a fair price, growth, or momentum? The kind of investor you are and sticking to the principles of your investment strategy is vital to know.

You are in the perfect location to learn more if you desire to be a value investor. Investment decisions should be founded, I believe, on valuation. Whatever tactics you use, a consistent approach is maintained. In other words, an investor in value should not be involved.

2. Invest with a Margin of Safety.

You have a margin of safety when you purchase an asset for less than its genuine value. One of my favorite words is Matters of prices! Investments that are below their actual or intrinsic worth are the best plan to reduce their risk.

If the conditions are favorable, a low price suggests an increase in upward gain. In the case of unconventional conditions, the low price also provides a safety margin. Something always goes wrong under less than ideal circumstances.

3. Asset Allocation is #1.

Your investment allocation will be the primary influencer of your return on investment as you split your portfolio among different asset groups. Unfortunately, many investors fail because the asset allocation plan is little thought-out or effort.

You will suffer low long-term returns if you put your money into overvalued categories of assets. It is necessary to overweight asset categories that are priced and underweight or to avoid costly asset categories.

4. Diversification is Vital.

The diversification of investment in small numbers offers enormous advantages. In other words, five investments are far superior to two; 10 are better than five investments. However, as the numbers are more than the expenses, the marginal benefits of adding extra investment are decreased.

In portfolio management, both diversification and diversification are common errors. The majority of research demonstrates the optimum of individual investments between 15 and 30.

5. Invest For the Long Term.

Short-term investment is one of the most significant declines in contemporary investment strategies. Really big investors appreciate that it can take time for the market to appreciate its true value if you buy an investment at a reasonable price.

A long-term investment is a fundamental investment principle because short-term trade often leads to low long-term output. This is prevalent because many investors allow fear and covetousness to lead them to unwise decisions. If you make sensible investment decisions, you will take care of yourself in the long run.

6. Keep Expenses Low.

Most investors do not understand how much their portfolios make a difference. Take a look at the 1 percent greater expense ratio of your returns.

Assume:
1. - $100,000 for 30 years lump sum investment.
2. -6,5% actual return rate minus 0,4% self-directed investor expense ratio.
3. -6,5% real return rate less 1.4% cost ratio for high-fare investors.
4. =Real return rate for self-determined portfolios increased to $590,829 by 6.1 percent.
5. =The real return rate for high charge investors of 5.1 percent increases to 444,715 dollars.
6. The gap is over 146,000 dollars!!!

In other words, during a 30-year period, your portfolio may cost 1% higher than the original investment!

7. Use Compounding to Your Advantage.

The powerful financial conception is compounding or exponential growth (they mean the same thing). Understand how this works for you and why the compounding of dividends increases the value of compounding.

The destruction of reverse compounding is vital to grasp. The more you lose your portfolio, the more difficult it is for you to return, as your principal is lost. A 10% loss only requires an 11% gain in order to return to a breakthrough. However, a loss of 50% requires a gain of 100% to return to the disadvantage.

8. Employ Risk Management Strategies.

As it is vital not to lose your principal, you need to utilize tactics for risk management. The return-of-investment killer is portfolio volatility. You will suffer a lot in bad markets if you don't control risk. Therefore, one of your key investment principles should avoid significant portfolio drawdowns.

9. Anticipate Market Volatility and Make it Your Friend.

Despise volatility but include volatility in the market. Portfolio volatility can be controlled, but the unavoidable volatility of financial markets cannot be monitored.

You should therefore be prepared to use investment opportunities. But, at the same time, if the conditions are unfavorable, you need to be aware of overestimated assets and eager to cash.

10. Control Your Own Destiny.

Nobody cares more than you do about your money. Unfortunately, fraud, interests, and unbelievable charges on Wall Street make a tempting option for self-directed investment.

Transaction costs have been lowered by technology and the internet and can obtain very low information and guidance. Therefore, there has never been a better time period for the self-directed investor who is ready to make some investment.

Criteria to Look For When You Invest In Dividend Stocks.

Dividend investments are a terrific strategy to construct your wealth. How dividend stocks function is to give owners part of the income in cash. It can be paid quarterly or annually. Shareholders can either utilize that cash dividend to fulfill their daily costs or reinvest some of that cash to purchase additional equities. The latter is usually the way to use the power of compounding interest.

Shareholders are reinvesting the dividends if part or all of the dividends are used to buy more equities. The reinvestment of dividends is a strong technique to increase your assets. You obtain cash from the shares and capital gains from raising the share price through dividends-paying stocks.

In the case of an annual return on dividends and an appreciation of equity of about 10 percent, the total return on investment for that term of 1 year is 13 percent. This return is much better than any other investment like bonds and fixed deposits.

You need to seek a few requirements in cash-paying firms before you go right to invest in dividend stocks. Here's a list of them to be careful about.

Revenue and Earnings Growth.

The income is the company's sales. This is the company's lifeline. The company would go bankrupt without sales and would pay the shareholders the cash dividend alone. Income is the amount remaining after expenses, taxes, loan interest, and so on have been born out of income. In a dividend-paying firm, both sales and revenue are essential measurements.

Ideally, you would like to see a rate exceeding 10 percent growth for both these metrics. However, only a few well-managed firms can increase revenues and profitability on healthy terms.

Debt.

Debt is what the corporation borrowed from the bank or from investors to build the company. The high debt interest payment is a highly leveraged corporation with loads of debt. During the economic crisis, the corporation will have difficulties paying the installment. As a result, a dividend-paying corporation will usually reduce the shareholders' share or even most of the cash dividends in such a period.

You seek a stock with little debt or better debt-free ideally. The key here would be the debt-to-equity ratio or the debt-to-equity ratio. These figures tell you the debt's share and share a capital proportion.

Dividend Payout Ratio.

The payout ratio can be classified into two classes, the payout dividend to earnings ratio and the payout dividend to free cash flow ratio. These ratios show how much income or free cash flow is handed out as dividends. The riskier the equities are, the larger the number of such ratios.

A high ratio shows that the bulk of the income and free cash flow was given out in cash. You surely want a low ratio since the corporation will have enough areas to pay out income and free cash flow.

These ratios will be kept essentially unaltered by well-managed organizations or slowly lowered. These ratios should be checked in quarterly financial reports and compared yearly. Look at this rate and find out why this significant change is happening.

The preceding are only some of the requirements for investments in dividend stocks. In fact, you may wish to consider other characteristics such as the history of paying dividends and business prospects. But these are the fundamental elements I've discussed to get you started. In all things, it was one of the greatest or safest approaches to increase your assets in the long term to invest in dividend stocks.

How to Choose the Best Dividend Stocks and Other Forms of Investment for Future Retirement Plans.

What makes a long-term investment in a diversified portfolio of dividend stocks lucrative for retirement plans?

Repeatedly, dividend funds have shown great success and have even surpassed S&P 500 and SDFs. In truth, they continue to remain solid, although the markets for non-dividend companies are far too chaotic and unpredictable. Thus, the greatest method to tackle inflation over the years is to invest in dividend funds. This is how the actual worth of the amount initially invested can be preserved. It is more challenging to give better returns at the conclusion of each year if the dividends have naturally been reinvested without a break.

Dividend equities are indeed a far better choice than government bonds with limited opportunity to keep inflation in check. Although 300 of the 500 companies included in the S&P 500 raised their dividends during the beginning of the recession. Even during the 2009 recession, the dividends were valued, especially in sought-after economies such as healthcare, energy, telecommunications, etc.

Characteristics of Best Dividend Stocks.

Invest in those firms you understand best, i.e., exclude companies interested in a wide range of products and initiatives that make them far too comprehensive. Instead, choose companies that focus on one or two similar goods, like Gillette, which sells razors and toothbrushes. Also, ensure that the products under the business are constantly being demanded, as are recession-free products such as health, food, cigarette, and alcohol.

Ensure that the company has more than enough cash flow every quarter. It doesn't have to borrow from its very own reserve to make dividends, which may be too catastrophic, as this cannot continue the firm's growth and development. Make sure that the company doesn't have to increase its capital too often to continue. Also, ensure that it is not in debt.

Also, do not apply to those organizations that give a payout rate over 80% to those who are offering a payout ratio of 50 percent (calculated by dividing annual dividends by annual net income). Too many of the company's revenues would have to be reinvested to continue to expand and flourish.

Invest in ETFs or Mutual Funds for Dividend Stocks.

To invest in high returns, the most efficient investments you can make by means of a mutual fund or exchange fund traded funds or ETFs are your methods. However, the recent impermissible market has affected many dividend-paying corporate stocks. Due to the market difficulty, the management of several listed companies has been compelled to divide their shareholders or stop paying dividends completely. It is wise to include at least one common fund or ETF in your portfolio that includes dividend payment equities of rising economies like BRIC countries since the dividend rates can sometimes be even greater than those of the United States. For India, Russia, Brazil, and China, the BRIC economy is an acronym. Goldman Sachs would surpass the economic might of the present developed and prosperous countries in the world in the combined economies of the BRIC. The BRIC countries could rival only Mexico and South Korea from now on.

List of Dividend ETFs for long term investment for high future returns.

These are only some of the dividend ETFs that can attract you and your investment interest. However, you must be warned that there is no way to support them, as if you invest in them, you have no stake. This is entirely at your discretion. So, whether you are willing to retire with lots of money into your cases and choose an ETF dividend stock that best matches your understanding, analysis, and many more aspects before taking one for future investments, here they are for your reading pleasure:

- ETFs comprise the Global Select Dividend Index Fund (FGD) and the European Select Dividend Index Fund (FDD) Dow Jones STOXX.
- iShares Dividend ETFs, including the IDV and Dow Jones International Select Index Fund (DIF) (DVY)

- PowerShares Dividend ETFs include International Dividend Achievers Portfolio (PID) and High Yield Equity Dividend Achievers Portfolio (PEY).
- Claymore ETF dividends which include both the ETF (HGI) and Claymore/ Zacks Dividend Rotation ETF (HGI) (IRO)

Investment dividend stocks both internationally and in the United States have many such ETFs. If you consider all of your priorities carefully and analyze your investment opportunities in SWOT (strength, opportunity, threat analysis, and weakness) before taking the massive step towards wealth.
The College Dropout Mathematics Genetics software and newsletters enabled him to convert $1000 to $1M in just three weeks.

Now, if you're willing to take a risk or have surplus cash other than those invested in better dividend stocks, you can invest $500 in short-term investment and trade, such as in popular penny stocks. A genius from Mathematics invented software recently that can assist you in buying your own wealth from home like an experienced professional trader.

That gentleman traded in penny shares effectively to make his first million in one year by investing just $1000. Since then, he has shared his manner of operations with others who subscribe for helpful advice and stock alerts to his newsletters. His software was designed based on various elements, including mathematical psychology, permutational mathematics, statistics, technological analysis, etc. Anyone who subscribes to his pay or free newsletters can take his steps literally and see him go through them. Well, why not take a free trial and see whether it suits you at all.

Remember that penny trading stock is very volatile and hence too risky to trade, but it's also flying or driving an aircraft. Once you learn and practice, you too can find it entertaining and easy to trade in penny stocks. So go forward and gently create your riches; never be too confident of your brain or of your intuition; it would be too disastrous. Keep yourself up-to-date on what is occurring around you. Do not hide your head in the sand like a storm. The investors themselves are a risk. Investment is not dangerous. Taking a step by step learning from the commerce experts, always have control and address all your challenges.

How to Invest in Best Dividend Stocks and Pick Penny Stocks for Maximizing Returns.

How to invest in the best dividend stocks and pick penny stocks for maximizing returns by applying stock market technical analysis?

Best Dividend Stocks:

Some of the best and most well-known stocks on the stock market are traditionally dividend-producing stocks. The finest dividend shares are the ones that have been paying all their shareholder's regular dividends for many years. Over the years, these have been recognized to be of constant worth. Such payment dividends have a superior return and a minimum risk than the so-called growth funds in the past. The surest for long-term investments is such forms of stock.

It is no wonder that stocks that consistently give regular dividends are stable and mature compared with equities whose price patterns vary too often. However, potential these volatile shares are difficult to interpret because of their irregular conduct and are beyond the understanding of novices entering the stock market. You must rely on "professional" brokers and fund managers for guidance in these instances.

Even when markets are chaotic, the shares that offer dividends are less likely to be volatile. These are the most lucrative among conservative investors who do not want to spend their hard-earned money very much. While the value of such shares does not rise and decrease as much as most of the growth funds, even though the economies of markets are slow or bumpy, they continue to increase slowly. In the long run, the paying dividends after several years have outstripped all other investment firms on the share market, which were simultaneously sowed in the start stage.

After the sale of these shares at market prices, the amount received by the investor would then, at the end of the decade, ten or 20 years, be substantial if he had properly reinvested the dividends as well. Thus, it is little wonder that the safest and best pick among investors with long-term goals remains such dividend payment shares.

However, stocks of these kinds, particularly Blue-Chip firms, are prized unless markets, such as during the recession, have rightly brought them. You must also have enough money in place to expand your investments to thickly cover huge, diverse dividends, paying inventories of reputable firms from several possible sectors – energy, infrastructure, finance, defense, food, security, FMCG, etc.

Furthermore, after investing the fund, you must be willing to forget it because it continues to lay golden eggs constantly, and you do not intend at any time to extract, along with the dividends earned and reinvested, the principal sum of the lock over time. Therefore, it would raise $400 at current market values for every dollar put in shares over forty years ago. That means that one now had to buy $2500 in the best available diverse dividend stocks in the early 1970s to gain millions of dollars for the same quantity of shares. This is a considerable sum with which to withdraw.

Penny Stocks for Investment:

However, some people have very little investment money and wish to get their toes on the stock market. A better option for individuals with little money is to invest in penny stocks. If you are young and capable of investing $500 or less in a different portfolio of penny shares, perhaps at the beginning of your 20s or 30s, you might take the calculated risk of earning more from penny shares. You also can earn $20,000 within one year if you're prepared to learn the ropes and pursue the trend using specially developed inventory analysis software.

Although it is exceedingly dangerous to invest in penny stocks, this must tell you that it cannot be compared to reputable dividend stocks. Although the Penny inventory may be quite risky in a very short time, say, one or two days, one must remain attentive to maximize it and minimize loss. It's easy to learn, but you'll not overestimate and stop by having control over one's greed component.

Penny inventory trading is less than 5 USD a share of the OTC, and because of its low price, the other inventories of listed businesses in NASDAQ and NYSE are not supervised or scrutinized. These are listed in the OTCBB, and you require the expert service to provide credible information and guidance on companies providing penny trading stocks. However, it is sometimes difficult for the average man because of various limits, which can occasionally prove difficult and annoying.

An MIT masterpiece dropout software designed to capture millions of pennies from its inventory:

However, it may genuinely detect which companies do well and which have tremendous potential through the stock market technical analysis, with the aid of sophisticated software, and your home or workplace comfortability.

Recently, young talent in mathematics has invented this kind of program at MIT. He has developed an algorithm for building software for unique stock analysis, which raised him a million dollars in one year by putting only 1,000 dollars into penny shares in only 38 trades. The same program helps to select the finest stocks for dividends. The program examines numerous elements, including human psychology, for inventory analysis and study to identify what the inventories are demanding and potentially.

CHAPTER TWO.
Dividend Stocks.

Dividend inventories might be handy for increasing your investment portfolio when long-term wealth is rising. Moreover, a wise dividend investment may improve your income. Would you like to add dividend shares to your portfolio? Let's examine what you need to know more closely.

What are dividend stocks?

A dividend stock is a kind of investment that offers two options for wealth creation. You can make revenue through dividend payments if you own a dividend stock. Furthermore, the inventory might improve your net cash value over time. Essentially, every stock may be a dividend stock, provided it rewards its owners with a piece of the company's profit through dividends.

Dividends are an additional amount received by an investor if the stocks or bonds they invest in perform sufficiently well to deliver the dividend stock issued profit to the company. Many businesses pay dividends based on a share of their earnings, that is, the proportion that is split into the investors' stock. These companies share their gains with the buyers of stocks and assist them to remain in the company, and reward their investors. Know the basic inventory ideas when looking for dividend stocks.

Dividend stocks are less volatile because investors are more inclined to hold dividend shares in binary markets by paying out cash. In raging bull markets, dividend equities tend not to advance as rapidly as non-dividend equities. Also, dividend inventories do not shrink as fast as non-dividend inventories. As a result of limited economic growth, investors are now looking for protection from the negative.

Dividends are given out in respect of earnings per share so that the more actions you have in a given stock, the more dividends you receive. In the income season and when companies declare profits and profits or losses on dividend stocks, this is usually the case every quarter. Dividends are usually paid into a cash market account to enable you to withdraw them. Certain bonds or other investment options made via a money market account compensate for some dividends. These dividends are a sort of investment interest.

Stocks of dividends obtain tax treatment favorably. As a result of an amendment to the tax law in May 2003, the most stocks dividend is charged only at 20 percent. This indicates that investors can receive a higher income from high-yield dividend stocks than the current investment strategy in the money market account or the COD (Certificate of Deposit). This should provide investors with savings of over an estimated $100 billion. The tax adjustment has produced savings of approximately $30 billion for people until now.

Dividend stock dividend return: The dividend return is a 12-month following dividend divided by the company's current share price. Dividend stocks dividend return: Increased payouts enhance profit, and the increase in dividends usually boosts the share price. Companies with a great history of stock price rise often adhere to this strategy. Do your dividend research to see which enterprises are not continuously increasing dividends because, for other reasons, they want to use their surplus income.

Please note that the high returns are high because many investors consider them risky and are therefore not the preferred choice. You want high, but not too high, dividend stocks with equity risk. Buying pressure often simply pushes share prices up until the return falls closer to more realistic stock markets. Confident investors will set a guideline of 5 percent for their maximum acceptable dividend return. For more risky dividend holdings, others will push up to a maximum of 8 percent.

Reinvesting dividends is a reasonably easy means of generating more dividends (specific stock) or investment income. The investment is good enough to pay dividends, and the reinvestment means that you have more stock than before. It is advisable not to reinvest your equity dividends. This is most likely true when you hold a cash balance to benefit from a high-interest rate payable to your money market account. It's also true that you plan to pay yourself out when you receive dividends from short-term investments.

Strong banks have been good payors of dividends in recent years, but higher interest rates have pinched hypothecary profit margins, and demand for new mortgages has declined. Now, it is not enough for banks to wage dividend stocks aggressively. However, it is all right to engage with local or regional banks that have shown themselves to offer excellent benefits from the maintenance and household mortgages.

However, what's the gift? First, it is essential that the dividend be understood precisely to give an overview of what that stock type can deliver. Dividends are payouts or cash on the income of the company. Basically, the dividends are firm profits split between shareholders. It accounts for a modest share of total profits and is usually paid in cash. As indicated above, most businesses pay dividends on a quarterly basis. However, some are paying monthly dividends and annual dividends. Your dividends can be calculated at a fixed or a variable rate. This depends on the sort of stock you have invested in. Please note that firms are not required to pay on their inventories. However, they regularly pay preferred shareholders except in the event of a financial crisis.

Example of a Stock Dividend.

Colin owns and owns 1.000 shares of ABC Company. The ABC Company board of directors has recently announced a 10% equity dividend. If the current share price is $10 and 100,000 total share remains, what is the impact on Colin's 1,000 shares of a dividend of 10 percent?

1. Determine ABC Company's market capitalization:

$10 x 100,000 shares Equals $1 000,000(market capitalization)

2. Determine the increase in outstanding shares by an equity dividend of 10 percent:

100,000 shares x 10 percent = 10,000 share increases.

3. Identify the new outstanding total shares:

10 thousand + 100 thousand = 110 thousand shares.

4. Determine the share number now owned by Colin:

Colin had 1% (1,000/100,000) of the whole outstanding shares before dividends were issued. The proportion of ownership of Colin in ABC stays the same as the stock dividend granted to all shareholders. Colin therefore owns a

1% share outstanding or 1% x 110,000 = 1,100 of the new total shares. The figure is similar to the 10 percent share dividend increase in Colin's 1,000 shares.

5. Identify ABC Company's share pricing:

An equity dividend does not increase the market capitalization of a firm. The ABC company continues to have $1 million in market capitalization. ABC's stock price would be $1,000,000/110,000 = $9.09 with 110,000 total shares outstanding.

How Dividend Reinvestment Boosts Your Returns.

Dividends remain a significant factor in these developments, which can increase your overall return on investments. You are helping your portfolio profit from improved compounding effects when you reinvest dividend payments to buy more stock shares in your investment. Each dividend that you reinvest at a fundamental level enables you to further dividend payments in the future that may exceed your return on investment.

You should be invested in the S&P 500 index foundation. Your annualized average return on stock pricing gains alone would have been 4.2% for a total return of 136%. Very good. Your annualized return would have amounted to 6.2 percent if you reinvested all dividend payments back into the fund over the same time, with a cumulative return of 247 percent. With just dividends would have almost doubled your profits.

Use this to play with the numbers a little bit, and more dramatic results will be found. For example, in January 2021, say you invested 10,000 dollars in the S&P 500 index fund. Today, you would have $91,300 based alone on cost gains. However, add reinvestments to the dividend, and you would almost double or $180,000.

Tax Benefits of Dividend Investing.

Investing in dividends can provide income investors with important tax advantages. However, all dividends are not treated the same by the Internal Revenue Service (IRS). The dividends of 'qualifying,' the lower rate of long-term capital gains taxed, and 'unqualified' or 'ordinary' are taxed as regular income in two groups.

U.S. corporations have qualified dividends for most dividends paid. If the investor owns the equity for 60 days (in most situations), then dividend income is taxed at the long-term capital gains rate. Other dividends – Real Estate Investment Trust (REI) or MLP – are categorized as standard dividends and are taxed as regular income. Some of them are classified as ordinary dividends. Also, common dividends are paid by money-market and other cash-like securities.

Dividends in tax-advantaged retirement funds, such as IRA or 401(k), usually are not taxable until you cancel them.

How to Evaluate Dividend Stocks.

Dividend returns are one means of assessing excellent equities paid for dividends. Many services help investors locate highly profitable dividend shares; however, it can be misleading to go with the greatest dividend yield.

Imagine that you are considering a stock paying $5 in dividends per year and valuing $100 a share until recently. The corporation was under pressure, though, and its shares were down to 50 dollars – although it still pays $5 each year. Thus, the dividend yield would have doubled to 10 percent over 5 percent in a relatively short period. In this situation, the increased dividend return is not an indication of a strong corporation but a symptom of stress.

A firm with a falling share price may have troubles, and the dividends may have to be re-examined by its board. Reliability is, therefore, a critical feature in the collection of stocks paid for dividends. "Is this business safe enough to continue paying the promised dividends—and even slowly grow them over time?" you have to ask yourself. In which safe dividend inventories can be found, the Aristocrats Dividend companies collect stocks that have historically increased dividend payments over time. In specific industries, stocks, such as property and utilities, can also, on average, provide greater dividends.

The dividend payout rate, which eliminates volatile stock prices from the equation by comparing a firm's profit to its dividend payment by share, is another metric of solid dividend stock. For example, if a firm makes $2 per share and pays a $1 dividend per share in each quarter, its payout ratio is 50%.

Lower payout ratios should indicate sustainable dividends – alternatively, a low payout ratio could lead to an increased dividend for a corporation. Conversely, a greater than 100 percent payout ratio shows that a company gives back shareholders more money than it earns and may need to cut its dividend – or that its income is under stress. On the other side, a continually rising payout ratio could show that a firm is healthy and generates trustworthy profits in a mature sector.

How You Can Pursue Dividend Investing.

You could apply one of the following three tactics to generate income through dividends investment.

Focus on High Dividend Yields.

This is the traditional dividend investment plan. The emphasis here is on slowly expanding, established companies that provide great dividends with a lot of cash flow. Such investments are meaningful if you want to earn revenue immediately. Just remember that not everything is high yields. The firms may not see as much stock value rise as other firms with smaller dividend yields.

Choose High Dividend Growth.

Early entry means that investors can acquire more shares and ultimately receive greater dividends. Long-term investors can focus on purchasing shares in businesses that expand fast but now pay less than average dividends. This will not generate as much revenue in the short term, but the dividend yield is supposed to progressively increase as a corporation grows and matures. This makes a stronger long-term investing strategy because of the cheaper "cost of rates."

Pursue Dividend Capture.

A more active and practicable method of dividend income collection is dividend capture. With dividend collection, the dividend cannot be earned by holding shares of a company for an entire year. Instead, you swoop in and purchase them right before the dividend is paid. You sell them again after you are paid so you can purchase new stocks.

It is not as simple as it sounds: you have to own a stock before the ex-dividend date, usually two weeks before the dividend payment, to get an annual or quarterly dividend payment. Then you have to select when to sell the dividend following payment. The problem is that share values are variable and may become lower when the dividend is paid than when you purchased it.

Such a decrease in share prices can quickly erase your dividend money—or more. And although your share increases in value, dividend capture can yield short-term capital gains taxed at a more regular income rate if you're not investing in a tax-friendly retirement account.

Risks of Dividend Investing.

Each investment plan involves risk, and investment in dividends is no exception. However, dividends are never guaranteed the most significant risk. Companies can and will lower their payouts and even remove them. Some highly important old-guard inventories have been part of the Covid 19 pandemic, such as Dick Sporting Goods, Carnival, Wells Fargo, HSBC, Airbus, and Rolls Royce, among others.

Of course, divergence should always be the top priority for every investor. But unfortunately, some areas and types of enterprises requiring proper diversification are often ignored by someone who is too focused on dividends. For example, young, rapidly developing technology companies usually don't pay dividends. But more subtle hazards are involved.

Lack of diversity always leads to increased volatility for investors. In addition, dividend-only investors can overlook substantial value growth in the sectors that do not pay dividends or pay uncompetitive payouts.

How dividend stocks work.

Dividend stocks can be quickly utilized to create income or develop wealth for the long term. For a sustainable investment, each side of the equation is compulsory. The total return is known as the conjunction of the paid dividend and the share price.

Many investors benefit from dividend stocks' profit-producing characteristics even though dividends never represent a certainty. However, the increase in stock prices is also crucial to consider. You can get dividends based on the number of shares you hold as an investor in dividend stocks. Dividends are often paid on a trimester basis through the shareholder's brokerage account. However, the date and method of payment will be determined by each company at a certain level.

Subject to the Board of Directors' approval of the payment, the corporation pays dividends. When it comes to getting paid dividends, there are four crucial dates to be aware of. The first one is when the company's board of Directors announces its intention to distribute dividends is the date for the declaration. The corporation then declares responsibility on its books upon announcement by the Board of Directors. The Board of Directors announces the date of payment and record date. The registration date is essentially the day on which the firm determines who its shareholders are. The other key date is the ex-dividend date on which the stockholders receive the dividends. You need to purchase the shares before the ex-dividend date to receive any dividends. The last date is when the shareholders are paid for the dividends.

Understanding The Types Of Dividend Stocks.

You have to know the many types of stocks which are present before you purchase the stocks. Dividend stocks are of three kinds: low returns, medium returns, and high returns.

The low-yielding stocks are usually smaller than the average yield, 2% or less. It is exceedingly improbable under inflation that those stocks will survive. You may not receive monthly dividends by investing in them.

The medium yield stock; the average yields up to 3% over the regular index yield. These shares pay between 30% and 50% of their dividend profits. Monthly dividends can be received if you invest in companies with such stocks.

Inventories that yield higher than the average yield are high yields. If you're seeking a monthly income, these stocks are excellent for you.

Who should pay attention to dividends?

Only two categories of people need to pay attention to dividends: those who invest and those who plan to invest in the stocks that pay for dividends. The first group is simple. People that get dividends have a passive revenue source that they desire to keep.

The value-for-money ratio of a corporation provides more information than the organization's balance sheet. It is an excellent instrument to evaluate equity and return on investments overall. Current and future investors may use dividends to assess the health of a firm.

Sometimes firms fake their financial statements using the figures. Just Google's "Enron" example for a book of false accounts. It might be hard for a corporation to tell what is real and what is not if it manipulates its earnings to impress investors.

A firm cannot counterfeit dividends. Yes, companies with overly high returns can be found, but most have a legitimate financial performance measures. The longer a dividend company has, the more reliable your investment can be.

You should pay particular attention to your dividends when the tax season begins. You will only pay a 15% tax on them if you have eligible dividends compared with a 25% tax on regular revenue. If your revenue drops below 25%, then tax-free dividends will make your revenue highly efficient.

What types of dividends are there?

The dividend types are explained.

Most investors get a classic dividend. It goes to persons whose shareholdings are based on the company's profitability. You will find two other kinds of stock worth mentioning:

Cash dividends.

Investors may get multiple dividends. Investors receive a direct payment when a corporation generates enough revenue to pay dividends. Some people prefer cash for the payouts.

Let's tell you your own Nike stock. In February 2019, the sportswear company declared a trimester cash dividend. You would have received 22 cents per share if you owned an outstanding stock. Note that, even if you reinvest it, you still must pay cash taxes.

Stock dividends.

Would you like to avoid paying your dividend payments tax immediately? You may want a dividend for stocks. Some corporations offer dividend reinvestment schemes that allow investors to slightly lower the market price to buy additional shares in a company.

The corporation and its investors profit from the stock dividends. Stockholders earn stock in the company, and its cash balance must not be reduced. Only when investors sell their shares will they invest tax on stock dividends.

Property dividends.

Dividends in real estate when cash and equity dividends are zags. Property dividends distribute actual assets to investors, such as a subsidiary organization's property, goods, or shares. When a corporation produces a profit, investors usually receive money or shares.

To prevent diluting their share value, companies offer property dividends. Property dividends can also be an alternative until the company has enough money to pay. Bookkeepers record the payout at the asset's market price; however, investors may keep their property if they like.

Scrip dividends.

A scrip problem arises when a corporation generates new shares and grants them to investors for free. The corporation uses its cash to create new shares and pay the stockholder. The procedure is an alternative to the tender process.

Most firms will deliver a script dividend if the company does not have enough money to pay a conventional cash dividend. The problem with the script allows investors to pick if they want cash or stock. Although these payouts work in line with dividend reinvestment schemes, they do not impose brokerage or costs since they are not a reinvestment technically.

Liquidating dividends.

Dividends are liquidated when a corporation is partially or fully liquidated. One advantage is that stockholders are not subject to taxation. Liquidating dividends differ from cash, as they are immediately derived from operating earnings.

Corporate managers can sell and pay off their liabilities some or all of their casts. Companies usually provide liquidation dividends when the company is undervalued by management. Miller's Bakery management estimates that the company is worth 30 million dollars, yet the highest proposal is 20 million dollars.

Special dividends.

A special dividend, often referred to as additional dividends, is taken from its lack of recurrent payments. Companies provide it to shareholders on an irregular basis, generally with a higher payout than their shareholders. Most special dividends relate to a specific corporate event like sales of property.

For example, Red Bull GmbH from Austria sold over 6 billion cans of energy beverage in 2016, collecting 6.3 billion euros. A special dividend of EUR 500 million was paid in the following year by the corporation. In addition, Red Bull GmbH generally provides investors with a dividend of €263.4 million annually.

Preferred dividends.

People who own preferred shares receive a favorite dividend. When it comes to payments, the favored asset sets its owners first. If a corporation cannot pay its dividends to all investors, it will first compensate preferred members.

There are certain trade-offs between owning preferred dividends. Since most investors buy preference shares in significant groupings, they renounce their voting rights on specific topics of the corporation. For example, they have no say in how corporate decisions affect shareholders.

Also, larger yields are provided for preferred dividends. This significant payout makes them one of the main reasons investors buy preferred shares. Commercial companies typically pay at a predetermined rate each quarter.

Why dividends matter?

Not all stocks have to pay dividends, but a stable, trustworthy income stream offers the portfolio a pleasant ballast.

Dividends have an appeal when we look at the two ways to get paid for investment – capital gains and dividends. The potential for a stock capital gain is strongly determined by what the market is doing in a given year. Stocks can buck downward, but most do not. Stocks are downward. On the other hand, dividends are generally paid both up and down the broad market.

Dividend reliability is a significant consideration for considering dividends in stock purchases. None of the shares has to pay a dividend, but a consistently reliable flow of dividends gives good leverage to the return of a portfolio. For example, every year since 1891, the multinational consumer product Procter & Gamble paid a dividend. The stock price of Procter & Gamble has not increased every year since 1891. During those decades, stockholders who possessed the stock were compensated by paying a dividend. They didn't depend entirely to be paid on capital profits.

Payback on your initial investment.

Think of reimbursement as a safe-net method. The expanding supply of dividends hedges inflation and speeds up the return on investment. Nobody knows how the stock will work overtime but calculating a payback term assists in achieving your initial investment in a predicted baseline performance – or worst-case situation. More investors are looking at two stocks and choose the most upside-down over time. All this focuses on recompense. The calculation of a stock repayment is based on the dividend flow following question: How long would it take for the dividend payments to rescue me from my initial investment if it does not make me money in value for money?

Look at the following example to grasp the concept of reimbursement. Let's imagine you're purchasing 200 $40 shares. Your investment will cost 8,000 US dollars, and your share will pay an annual dividend of 1.20 US dollars (3%). Based on this dividend, you estimate $240 in dividends in the first year. When your initial $8,000 investment in approximately 33 years goes by, if that income stream doesn't alter. What if the dividend stream increased by only 5% annually? In 20 years, you will recover your initial investment. This would shorten your payback period by roughly 13 years, in other words.

The change in the stock price over time does not influence this estimate. Over time, the stock return is not affected. It just presupposes that your initial investment should be recovered by a single assumption – a projected increase in dividends.

Should you concentrate on equities with the fastest return? Not necessary. Not necessarily. The total return is ultimately important. It's nice to have an equity payback in just 15 years, but it is preferable to have equity five times your initial investment in 15 years. Nevertheless, dividend paybacks are a helpful notion to frame two stocks' risk-return potential. The payback matrix enables the payback period (for years) to be determined based on dividend returns and the assumptions on dividend growth.

The relationship between dividends and market value.

Dividend-paying companies provide an opportunity for investors to pay during rough periods when it is difficult to make financial gains. They offer a decent safeguard from inflation, particularly if they expand over time. In contrast to other sources of income, such as interest on fixed revenue investments, they are tax advantages. The average shareholding in dividends is usually lower than that of non-dividend shares. And a dividend stream can help develop enormous wealth over time, especially when it is reinvested to benefit from the power of compounding.

But dividends are expensive. Unless its market value is affected, a corporation can pay dividends to shareholders. Consider the finances of your own. If you pay family members money frequently, your net value will fall. For a corporation, it's nothing else. Money paid to shareholders by a firm is money that is no longer a component of the company's asset base. The funds cannot be used more to reinvest and expand the enterprise. The decrease in the "rich" of the firm must indicate a decreasing stock price adjustment.

When a dividend is paid, an inventory price adjusts lower. The change cannot easily be detected in the middle of daily price changes in ordinary stock, but the change occurs. This change is significantly more apparent when an enterprise provides a "special dividend" (also known as a one-time dividend). When an enterprise pays its shareholders a special dividend, the equity price is reduced instantly.

The ex-dividend dates.

The stock price adjustment occurs on the ex-dividend day. The ex-dividend date is typically two working days before the registration date. The date for the ex-dividend is the cut-off for the dividend. In order to get the next dividend payment, you must have stock before the ex-dividend date. You are not entitled to the next paid dividend if you purchase stock on or after your ex-dividend date. Recall that the stock price adjusts downwards to reflect the dividend payment if it sounds unjust. Thus, you pay a lower share price if you acquire on or after the ex-dividend date, although you are not entitled to a dividend.

Why Is Dividend Investing So Popular?

Once upon a time, people never invested in shares. Bonds, bank accounts, and GICs earned considerable interest, so equity acquisition was not essential. With inflation and interest rates falling, people began to look for different ways to create income for an extended period and stayed low. Rent from real estate and dividend investment are two of the most popular options. Investment in real estate entails acquiring and renting properties and is not further explored in this report. This section explores dividends investment through the purchase of shares.

When it comes to dividend investments, it's important to remember.

Dividends are Not Guaranteed.

Most individuals are aware of the failure to guarantee equities and mutual funds unless Canadian deposit insurers apply. This is usually the case if your investment institutions go insolvent. The same applies to reciprocal funds as to dividends. An enterprise may change or cancel its dividend payment without much warning. This is generally reported at meetings of shareholders and through press announcements. It is true that businesses that discard or cut dividends tend to acquire poor market publicity, therefore preventing them from doing so, but this is still true. If dividends are slashed, this could influence the path of the company. A scenario is feasible when a corporation decides to put a lot of idle cash into a new product, a new business line, or another firm that needs money to thrive. The corporation has now decided to conserve the money and allow capital gains to be generated instead of paying dividends. A second situation is that the enterprise does not make as much money as previously and can no longer pay dividends. A third case is when a firm is adversely affected by a change in regulation like litigation, a merger, a takeover, or a natural disaster that causes the company to modify its dividends trajectory. Scenarios also exist when dividends rise higher than anticipated, including unanticipated additional profit, a one-time dividend payment arising from an acquisition contract, a court win, or a change in legislation favoring a company that results in a substantial increase in profit. Read the media reports and interpret the present scenario to determine what is happening in an enterprise.

Dividends May or May Not Keep Up With Inflation.

Every year, several enterprises increase dividends. In other circumstances, this is anticipated since it has been happening for many years. These increases are designed to maintain dividend revenue constant, with the rising stock price rising and paying additional money for each share in your stock. These greater repayments keep your investment up to inflation and maintain its value for a long time. This situation will not be up to inflation as you would receive the same amount in the dollar over many years if your share price is stable and the dividend payments remain unchanged. With rising prices, you will realize that your money is purchasing less and less and that it squeezes cash. This issue is especially critical if you only receive dividends or live on a set sum of money. This category includes many senior citizens and those with fixed-state assistance. To learn what happens in this instance, check the payout history for the company you invest in and determine if payout increases may be expected. When most of them are predictable, but the trend is changing unexpectedly, find out what happened to the company at that moment. These periods will determine the stock's reliability when paying dividends.

Dividend Yields are Inversely Affected by the Stock Price.

A percentage called a 'dividend return' is given to you by the dividend dollar amount received divided by the share price at the time of the dividend payments. This computation compares that return with other investments, such as bond yields or GIC yields. This output can be compared over time to see the scope of the output. Since this computation is based on the stock price, the proportion you receive or the rent of the dividend would decrease as the price of the stock increases. In contrast, this dividend yield would increase when the share price falls. This wouldn't matter to you if you invest in a steady income and hold the shares already if you wish to shift investment or if you require some principle (money invested) as an alternative to the ownership of dividend stocks. This return compares if you invest new money into dividend stocks to inform you if the stock you wish to purchase is either "cheap" (high profit) or "cheap" (the yield is low). There is much that affects stock prices; therefore, this return will fluctuate significantly at a given period based on inventory prices. Unless there is something unique - as mentioned in the previous paragraphs - the dividend payment would not fluctuate significantly.

What About Interest Rates?

When investing in dividend-paying stocks, interest rates should be closely monitored. The higher the interest rates, the more likely it becomes to sell dividend shares since someone may purchase an alternative that is bonds or other securities that bear interest. It's like a substitute effect – you buy a cheaper version of the thing if one thing becomes very costly and a more affordable version of it is produced. In this situation, you are likely to purchase your dividend stock after assessing the risks, costs, and taxes if a dividend stock provides you with a 5% income stream and a bond provides you with a 2% revenue stream. If the bond gives you a 4% revenue stream because of increased interest rates, this dividends stock is not enticing. Then if the bond returns an income stream of 6 percent, the dividend paid out share will now have a greater return. People would then sell the dividend stock until the price drops to close to 6%, or an equivalent return after risk, costs, and taxes. Since the dividend payout will not change so fast, the market's only choice is to modify the price – in this case, the dividend stock's price – in balance with both possibilities.

The Mechanics of Dividend Investing.

So what are the dividends you are getting? Traditionally, a trading account should be opened with a bank, investment company, or stockbroker. The account must be such that individual stocks can be purchased. These stocks can be bought by yourself or somebody else. Before starting the account, make sure you ask questions about prices, restrictions on account access, and taxes. In each individual corporation, you would purchase shares. For example, 100 Bell Canada Enterprises shares would be purchased (BCE's trading symbol). This would cost you an example, $50 per share. If you acquire 100 shares, $5,000 plus any charges for buying the shares is invested. Some accounts also have charges to keep your account open, so ask questions before purchasing your inventory because these charges will lower your money. You're entitled to a dividend payment on a quarterly basis once the shares are in your name. The fourth end date is the quarter end date of the company and not necessarily the quarter end date of the calendar. If you own the shares, the name of your company's name and the name of a brokerage account, the name of an account holding the shares will be scheduled to receive the payment when the day of payment of the dividend is approaching. You'd receive the dividend if you purchased shares before that date. In your account, where the shares are housed, you would notice a cash payment. In some circumstances, you can reinvest dividends in more shares rather than cash to ensure that you keep buying more shares, not yourself. By doing this, it is a great way to increase your inventory. If you wish to use the revenue, this is not to be done because shares must be sold regularly to create cash, which would entail numerous transaction costs and problems to ensure your business gets the best price. In addition, it's quite hard to time the market, which should be avoided if you don't have some knowledge.

When Should You Not Invest in Dividends?

The answer to this will depend on your motives for the first-time buying dividend returns and your risk tolerance. If you want income and can purchase bonds to earn that income, the latter will be a safer bet. If you risk losing your money, and a guaranteed alternative investment is made for you, you should instead buy the guaranteed alternative. You can desire to maintain your dividend stocks if you love dividend income and like your capital gains, even if you have other choices. Where interest rates climb abruptly, and you lose your dividend stocks heavily, the whole idea of dividend investment can be turned off. Investing in real estate is the route for you if you love the immovable and generate equivalent revenue from real estate instead of dividends investment. You are better aware of how things function.

How to Tie This All Together.

Dividend investment should always be considered together with everything else, financially and otherwise, in your life. Note what you want with the investment of dividends, your possibilities, and how comfortable you are with each alternative. You should also take into consideration the quantity of knowledge you have about each opportunity. The more you know, the better you'll be at it. When you know little about something, take it as an experiment and wade in carefully with any support until you know a lot.

Why Do You Need to Be Investing in the Best Dividend Stocks Out There Right Now.

You miss out on an enormous best dividend stock when you're not hunting for the greatest dividend shares. In the beginning, the entire object of stock was to make dividends payable to their owners.

Over the years, interest in these inventories has risen and declined. There has been a renewed interest since 2002, yet it is still not as popular as it should be. It should be essential for you to because it is an excellent time to invest in it.

Dividend shares provide both growth and income. The following are some reasons why you should take this into account:

1) They give out a good return.
2) Dividends are taxed only slightly. Here, we are only talking about 15%. This is quite significant compared to other possibilities.
3) They just send it to you; you have nothing to do to earn your dividend! Less work, I like to do.
4) You have a lot more control over them; the funds aren't "trapped" like many other investments. Dividend stocks give you flexibility over your investment.
5) Over time, dividends might increase (unlike bonds). This can drastically enhance your income.

6) Overtime also, dividend returns may increase. Again, this can considerably compound your income.

As you can see, some unique traits of the top dividend stocks tend not to have in other investments. They are fortunately relatively easy to buy. You must apply common sense, like all other things, and not just buy the first stock you will find.

Best Dividend Stocks to Buy.

But with growth reserves now considerably more available as the economic recovery is beginning, a continuous value rotation is on track. 2021 has been significantly more stable than its turmoils predecessor. And, despite the account of increasing concern over the steady increase in the 10-year Treasury income, it remains below 1.7%, which is historically incredibly small. This means stocks with high dividend incomes continue to have a stronger attractiveness than average. This is the finest dividend share for 2021 - every December, the year ahead is the annual list of the USA News & World Report. There have been only two of the next 15 stocks of dividends.

Target Corp. (ticker: TGT)

First, Target is on the list. Maybe its 1.3% dividend return leaves something desirable for most investors but is confident because it is only two in 15 options with less than 2%. The objective is an excellent 2020, where its stock continues to reap the benefits of its enhanced attention to digital sales. In 2017, Target launched a multi-year $7 billion investment strategy to be more numerical and pay off big time. Digital sales of 118% climbed last quarter following a 155% rate in the previous quarter. At just 31 percent, its payout ratio was small, showing that the dividend is safe and has the capacity to expand. TGT's earnings are only 31 percent.

Greif (GEF)

As the smallest firm on this list, Greif can offer a dividend portfolio of mid-cap diversification through a market capitalization of approximately 3 billion dollars. This is a little growing company, but the GEF provides an excellent combination of income and steady growth with a 2.7-percent dividend and analysts forecasting profits per share (EPS). The world economy is recovering, which means it already benefits from improving demand for this steel and plastic drums manufacturer, corrugated sheets, containers, and other packaging items behind the scenes. Greif's products are used by many industries, including just a few customers in the pharmaceutical, petroleum, food, drink, and chemical industries.

AbbVie (ABBV)

AbbVie is a pharmaceutical company that reached the list in 2020 and is a repeat pick of the 15 top dividend stocks. Last year ABBV's stock won a surplus, adding approximately 28 percent by 2020. AbbVie sells in Humira, which cures numerous conditions, including arthritis, Crohn's disease, and plaque-psoriasis, the world's largest blockbuster medicine at a market valuation of over 200 billion dollars. In addition, the Botox Maker Allergan acquisition, which was finalized in mid-2020, contributes to further diversifying its portfolio. ABBV pays an exceptional 4.5 percent dividend.

JPMorgan Chase & Co. (JPM)

2020 was a year down for the banks. Interest rates plummeted, reducing the critical divide between the money a bank pays for borrowing and the credit rates. Even JPMorgan Chase & Co., the most precious bank in the United States, had not been immune to the headwinds. This was a fantastic purchasing opportunity for patient investors seeking a safer asset with decent returns. JPM and other bank equities have profited from much higher interest rates in the early 2021s; the JPMorgan equity handsomely beats this year's market and still provides a dividend of about 2.2%. In the last quarter, JPMorgan recorded a 25% increase in commercial turnovers, a 32% increase in deposits, and a 28% growth in managed assets. The 29 percent payout ratio shows plenty of space for the dividend to increase.

Johnson & Johnson (JNJ)

The health care company Johnson & Johnson is another one of the few recommendations from 2020 repeated in the Best Dividend Stocks to purchase for 2021. As AbbVie did, JNJ shares did not do in 2020, increasing approx. 11%. Johnson & Johnson, a decades-long children's blue-chip inventory, operates in three divisions: medical devices, consumer products, and drug products. The consumer, who sells all from Listerine, and Tylenol to Pepcid and Band-Aids, is basically bulletproof and fine. The medical equipment division was responsible for the decrease in weaknesses by 2020, and segment sales decreased by 10.5% as hospitals were scaled back on pandemic surgery. However, it already began to bounce back in the first quarter, and JNJ's most significant pharmaceutical business increased last quarter by 7.4 percent.

Iron Mountain (IRM)

On this list, Iron Mountain is the first property investment trust, or REIT, specializing in storage and information management services. The company thrives as it embraces the digital age more and more. The company claims that over 225,000 international organizations have saved and protected billions of dollars in assets. As REIT, it can avoid double taxation through the legal structure of IRM. It has to give its shareholders 90% of its taxable income, but it does not pay corporate tax in exchange. As a result, Iron Mountain should be taken into account by investors ready to favor reliable revenues above significant growth potential. Among all 15 equities in this list, the top performances were equities with a pretty tight market range of 2021 and currently yield 5.9 percent.

PepsiCo (PEP)

PepsiCo, a corporation with exceptional diversification in regions and business sectors, also has the greatest beverage and snack shares to buy for 2021. In 12 weeks concluded on March 10, the Frito-Lay division of Frito-Lay North America accounted for 28.6% of total revenues, not far behind its top 34.3% PepsiCo Beverage segment of North America. His greatest adversary, the Coca-Cola Co. (KO), has a robust food and snacks sector. And although EPS was 19% down in Coca-Cola's previous quarter, PepsiCo's EPS was 29% up. PEP is a dividend of 2.9%. Despite its disappointing performance up to now, Pepsi is a consistent, good long-term holding, a best-in-class stock compared to Coca-Cola.

Discover Financial Services (DFS)

The Discover Financial Services credit card firm lists the top 15 dividend holdings which can be purchased for a second consecutive year. DFS is the smallest of the four leading credit Card firms with a value of around 35 billion dollars, including Visa, 497 billion dollars (V), Mastercard, 357 billion dollars (MA), and Americ Express, 125 billion dollars (AXP). In some ways, this provides DFS with more market share on the table than other corporations. The biggest dividend for the four firms, DFS, also pays 1.5 percent. The pay-out ratio for DFS is relatively small. Credit cards should generally continue to increase their market share versus alternative payment methods by 2021 as more business goes online and away from cash.

Cisco Systems (CSCO)

A 2.8 percent dividend with a payout rate of 60% is paid off at $223 trillion from Cisco, a blue-chip company component of the Dow Jones Industrial Average. The corporation raised its dividend for nine consecutive years and remained an actual cash cow through the pandemic. Last quarter alone, non-GAAP operating cash flow climbed 2% year-on-year to $4.1 billion.

Thus, the communication equipment company, which essentially produces a large proportion of the plumbing that enables the internet, should be a reliable, long-term dividend investment. Even last quarter, through stock purchases and dividends, Cisco returned stockholders $2.3 billion.

Mondelez International (MDLZ)

For numerous reasons, these 87 billion dollars in snack food titanium are among the best dividends for 2021. First, the enterprise is relatively steady, which most investors desire to see in their dividend shares. Mondelez has extensive brand recognition and loyalty with various brands, including Oreo, Cadbury, Toblerone, Halls candie, Trident gum, and Tang powdered drinks. Second, Mondelez is a wonderful method to expand your portfolio internationally, with 73 percent of its revenue coming out of North America last quarter. MDLZ pays a dividend of 2% and has a payout ratio of 46%.

Crown Castle International Corp. (CCI)

Crown Castle International Corp. is the second-largest REIT of the top dividend shopping stocks for 2021. More than 40,000 cell towers are owned, operated, or leased in the United States in an increasingly vital niche sector. Its property covers all major U.S. markets, and CCI is an investment in the essential communications infrastructure that keeps the Americans linked to information, data, and one another. CCI towers will also be a significant part of the implementation of 5G – or fifth-generation technology – in years to come. CCI provides a dividend of around 3%.

AT&T (T)

Without discussing AT&T, you cannot talk about the biggest telecom firms in this country. It is the second-largest telecom corporation in the United States, but it also has a massive media empire valued at roughly 30 billion dollars. This is behind Verizon Communications (VZ), including CNN, Warner Bros., TBS, HBO, TNT, DC Comics, Cinemax, etc. AT&T will also play a central role in implementing 5G tech. The company's unprecedented choice, called "The Many Saints of Newark," will simultaneously be released for streaming on its HBO Max platform. In addition, it provides 17 theatre releases – including "Space Jam: New Legacy," "The Matrix 4," and "The Sopranos," which is the film prequel to the company. Recently, a deal was negotiated with Discovery (DISCB) to consolidate its media assets into a separate publicly traded firm. AT&T pays a savvy dividend of 6.5%.

Antero Midstream Corp. (AM)

Whenever you notice an increase of around 9.8% in a dividend so high as Antero Midstream, the alarm bells will go out. Usually, with this picture, something is amiss. Whether the dividend should be lowered, the company would tumble freely, or another risk would arise. Antero Midstream, therefore, seemed like one of the riskiest stocks on this list at the beginning of the year. At 4.7 billion dollars, it was the second smallest enterprise on the list, but it was also unprofitable in 2020 since it was only beginning to reverse the impact in gas prices, which covered much of the last year. A global recovery from the epidemic resulted in an energy price bull market and the stock price of AM.

Newmont Corp. (NEM)

Newmont Corp. was definitely named one of the top ten shares of U.S. News to purchase for 2021, and it also earned a place on this list. The gold, silver, and coffee mine produces a small 3.1%, but it has pledged to give special dividends to shareholders if its mining operations produce unexpected gains. Newmont has an attractive value as a hedge in recessionary conditions because of its low correlation to the broader market. NEM's beta is incredibly low at 0.29, a measurement that showed perfect market correlations at one and no market correlations at zero. Newmont plans to spend between $800 and $1900 on mine an ounce of gold by 2025. Gold is worth over 1 800 dollars an ounce now.

Dividend Stocks and How to Invest in Them.

Dividend stocks can be an excellent investment for investors searching for consistent income.

Are you looking for a recurring revenue investment? A wise choice can be high-dividend stocks.

Dividend inventory regularly distributes to investors a piece of the company's income. (It is also possible for investors to reinvest the dividends. More about dividends and their working methods.) most US dividend shares pay a quarterly sum to investors, while the top investors increase their payment to help investors create a cash stream like an annuity.

Dividend-paying enterprises are often well established so that dividend shares can increase your portfolio stability. This is one reason why they are listed on our low-risk investment list.

Investing for income:
Dividend stocks vs. dividend funds.

There are some significant ways to invest in dividend stock: mutual funds, including index funds or foreign exchange funds, which have dividend holdings or buy dividend shares.

Dividend ETFs or index funds give an investor access in a single investment to the dividend stock selection, which means that you can only hold a dividend stock portfolio with one transaction. The fund will, after that, regularly offer you dividends that you can earn or reinvest. In addition, dividend money offers an immediate diversification benefit – you can always count on income from others if one stock held by the fund drops or suspends its dividend.

Whether through dividend stocks or dividend funds, your return on investment may be considerably enhanced if these dividends are reinvested; payouts often raise a stock or dividend fund's return by some percentage points. For instance, the total yearly return (including dividends), on average of around two percentage points, of the S&P 500 has been more significant than the annual change in the value of the index.

And it can build up to that difference. For example, we can see that an investment of $5,000 which has grown at six percent a year for 20 years, might increase to almost $16,000 using NerdWallet's investment calculator—increasing dividends by up to 8% and $5,000 to more than $24,000.

Generally speaking, an excellent idea is to put the bulk of your portfolio in index funds for the following reasons. Yet direct investment in dividend shares has advantages. While the investment needs more work — in research on each stock to ensure that it fits into your entire portfolio — investors who select individual dividend shares can create a customized portfolio that can deliver a higher return than a dividend fund. Expenditure with dividend stocks can also be reduced as ETFs and index funds charge investors with an annual fee known as a spending ratio.

It takes time and commitment, but it's worth it for many investors to build a portfolio of individual dividend equities. Here is how a dividend stock can be purchased:

1. Find a dividend-paying stock. On numerous financial sites and on the web of your online broker, you can screen for shops that offer dividends. A list of high-dividend stocks is also listed below.

2. Evaluate the stock. In the first place, the dividend yield among its pairs is comparable with a high dividend stock category. If the dividend return of a company is far higher than that of similar businesses, it can be a red indicator. More investigation into the company and the security of the dividend at least is worthwhile.

3. Then check at the payout ratio of the stock, which shows you how much the company earns dividends. A too high payoff ratio — often over 80%, even if it might vary according to industry — suggests that the company pays dividends for a substantial proportion of its revenues. In rare situations, the payout ratio of dividends might reach a maximum of 100%, which means that the corporation can be in debt to pay dividends.

4. Choose how much stock you would want to purchase. When buying individual stocks, you need diversity to determine how much your portfolio enters every stock. For instance, you can buy 20 equities, and you can add 5% of your wealth. If your stock is nonetheless riskier, you may wish to buy less of it and make safer selections for more of your money.

The security of its dividend is the first consideration in purchasing a dividend stock. Too high a dividend return may suggest that the payout is unsustainable or that investors sell the company, reduce their share price, and so increase the dividend yield. Dividend yields above 4% should be studied carefully, with over 10% tackling dangerous zone firmly.

Things you must consider Before Investing in Dividend Stocks.

1. **Investment objectives.**

Each investor should take certain financial objectives into account. Risk appetite, financial resources, and time horizon for investment are involved. Investment targets are essential for investors to select appropriate investment options – dividend inventories in this situation.

2. **Choice of dividend stock/s.**

Dividend inventories are difficult to select as investors may not know where to start. However, investors can have vital insight into stock prices by offering market value. This can help investors identify value and growth stocks and make comparisons between stocks and across stock or market capitalizations possible.

3. Dividend ETFs.

Dividend investment may not only mean the purchase of individual shares. Dividend ETFs that provide exposure to a large selection of dividend-paid shares can also give you access to dividend shares. The components of the ETF must be viewed to verify that the ETF complies with the requirements for the dividend stock, as some ETFs may contain other components such as bonds, commodities, etc.

4. Dividend history.

The choice of stock on the higher proportional dividend alone may appear to be the apparent theoretical option, but it is necessary to have an overall strength and prospect. For example, a firm can issue a large dividend, but it can be essentially unstable with a dark future. This could reduce or possibly altogether abandon the company's dividend payments in the future. This shows the necessity of appropriate analysis and research rather than the greatest return on dividends.

The compilation of a list of high-end dividend stocks might be a solid starting point for investors to buy and not buy stocks after a thorough dive into each firm.

5. Brokerage allowance and reinvestment options.

The choice of the most appropriate broker is steadily ignored, but it can affect the investment's easy transaction, cost, and appropriateness. An easy-to-use platform is vital not to mislead investors, especially rookie investors.

Investors must comprehend how inventories work as far as order kinds, bourse cash, trading hours, and volumes are concerned. These simple notions benefit investment decision-makers. Costs play a significant role since commission costs can be used to assure potential profits before committing to investigate likely brokers.

As previously indicated, dividend reinvestment (DRIP) can significantly influence the dividend investment strategy. Unfortunately, many brokers are not providing this service; therefore, please check this ability with your broker or prospective brokers.

How to Invest in Dividend Stocks.

It is crucial to understand what entails dividend investment, but it may be harder to utilize this knowledge in an investment selection. An easy variant of the dividend stock analysis is the hypothetical example below.

Dividend yield.

The share price of Company A is approximately 2.4x that of Company B in this scenario. This reflects a similar 2.8x dividend proportion. Thus, company A has shown a greater dividend yield based on the recent dividend disbursements in percentage terms.

However, higher dividend returns do not always reflect excellent investment possibilities because declining stock prices might inflate these higher dividend yields. Unfortunately, this doesn't appear accurate, as the % change YTD makes it plain that the prices of both Company A and Company B have fallen below Company A's pricing.

Future expectations are the primary issue, and one of both companies feels an investor has more potential for growth, therefore providing the possibility of higher dividend payments on the road.

P/E ratio.

The P/E ratios of both banks are like that of Company A, indicating that investors pay more for every dollar of Company A's income. This could be owing to higher dividend returns or, perhaps, investors expect Company A to have more significant potential for growth compared to Company B. Recall that the P/E ratio is merely a snapshot of the share price of a firm divided by income; hence, only one analytical piece of the pie.

Payout ratio.

With Company B, the payout percentages are again like company A. These percentages indicate to investors how much the company earns dividends. But, again, a very high payout ratio could be concerning since it shows a lack of faith in growth plans by this company.

Dividend growth YoY.

In this example, the latest dividend growth criteria YoY Reveal Company A (9.83 percent) was well above Company B (1.08 percent). Together with the increased dividend return, this might make company A look more attractive with only these few consideration variables, comparable YTD movements, and similar P/E ratios.

However, it is crucial to remember that many other variables need to be considered when selecting an investment, such as management, growth expectations, market positioning, etc.

Investors must ensure adequate risk management with any financial action and function in accordance with their financial situation. In this regard, the entire market positioning and factor in global (economic and political) potential stimuli for prudent investment decisions must also be considered.

CHAPTER THREE.
How Can You Lose Money Investing in Dividend Stocks?

Many naturally assume that investing in dividend shares is a sure way of gaining money, primarily if you invest, for example, in those with large payouts of 5% to 10%. That's not accurate at all, however.

You can argue that the time of your picks does not necessarily matter if you invest in a 10- or 20-year period. That's because 5% of your dividend stocks annually make those payments more than compensate for any flat or somewhat negative price changes in your share. This is because This is especially true when the revenues are reinvested annually.

If you don't want to hold such stocks, if this is the case, you have to focus more on when you buy since this might make a significant impact. If a company is expected to continue to provide substantial dividends annually, you should preferably invest in those enterprises if the stock price is over-sold. For example, when indicators like RSI and Stochastics are both oversold.

You can have higher capital gains when you sell, and you will also gain more from your dividend payments in percentage terms. To show this point: if the equity dividend is

10p per year, if you bought 100p, you would get 10% per year, if you purchased 6.66% at 150p, and if you bought at 200p, only 5%.

You might quickly lose money from these companies in the long term if you have a history of buying companies when they are strong, which can frequently prove to be the most important trend. In the interest of getting good dividends, there is little purpose in investing if you purchase at high prices. Afterward, the share price could fall considerably, thereby offsetting the benefit of income that you receive annually.

You can quickly lower or scrap your dividend if you face problems. You can also lose money if you're looking for tiny and medium-sized enterprises for income-generative stocks. Although several of these companies provide very attractive returns, their futures are far riskier than many major holdings because they are much less safe.

Therefore, the argument is that even if you invest for the long run, you are not assured money from high dividend companies. Yes, some vast businesses should have significant profits, but there is still a risk aspect. So, in the nearest future, that is something you may want to keep in mind.

Hazards to Avoid When Investing in Dividend Stocks.

Dividends are payments, either cash or shares, made semi-regularly to shareholders of a corporation. Dividend companies are usually very stable and well-established firms with robust operations but without much possibility for expansion. Thus, dividends are a way of investment in income since they provide a relatively safe and constant payment and are perfect for anyone seeking a more stable type of income.

Investing in dividends may be a big move, but a prudent investor must know a few problems. First, recent legislation has raised taxes, giving long-term investors significant advantages over those who regularly buy and sell dividend-paying investments. However, those investors who buy and retain must be prepared for market ups and downs. Another concern to investors is credit risk.

Credit risk. Credit difficulties can nonetheless be averted if the investor focuses on earnings and is prepared to sell when the firm does not measure itself. Finally, an investor will only deal with another potential problem, namely inflation risks, until the economy stabilizes.

Recently there have been surprisingly good results in areas including energy producers, infrastructure, and utility holdings. However, even if the three sectors did well, they are not guaranteed to be free of credit problems or other problems - and being overexposed in an industry may lead to huge losses if one industry were suddenly to decrease. There is a higher risk of loss by diversifying amongst different areas, but each loss is isolated, significantly reducing the overall damage. Overall, successful investments are more likely to lead to some modest failures depending on your chosen sector.

Dividends are a fantastic source of income investment, notwithstanding a few barriers that can be avoided. Although certain dangers arise, as dividend-based corporations tend to be well defined and steady, the risk is far smaller than for a rapidly developing company. In summary, dividend inventories are great for individuals looking for a more predictable source of income.

Stocks That Pay Dividends - Reasons Dividend Stocks May Be Right for You.

A continuous source of profit for your portfolio is an investment in equities that offer constant dividends. Investors that seek regular revenues from their investment portfolios or more constant returns from their stock investments can find appropriate alternatives to the stock that pays dividends. The following are some of the features of this investment income generating:

1. Stocks of dividends payable can be a single company, or many can be part of the holding company's structure, trust, closed-end mutual fund, ETF, etc. However, this should be noted that many businesses are not eligible to invest in the dividend simply because they do not pay dividends.

2. Dividend-paying companies do so since their management staff, and management boards decide, at discretion, to pay their shareholders a dividend on a deliberate and regular basis. While most businesses do so quarterly, there are several equities paying dividends monthly.

3. In general, dividend stock has policies that encourage continued dividend payments. While the management and the board of directors are therefore responsible for the decision to pay a dividend, they generally aim to run

the company in a way that safeguards and, in many cases, increase the income from the dividend to the shareholders over time.

4. In many cases, dividend-paying stocks are bigger and more established corporations (i.e., most are well-known and established businesses). As a result, they have established steady financial flows with highly predictable incomes. Utility companies, for example, are the main form of stock payable with a dividend, having a solid, predictable revenue source, understandable expenditure (typically carried on to consumers if expenses increase suddenly), leading to a reliable source of earnings with which to pay dividends.

5. The equities are volatile, but the dividend-paying equities are usually less volatile than the stock market overall. This is because investors are confident enough in their profitability and their owners' incomes on a regular basis that they reward this stability with lower price volatility, given that these holdings are reasonably seen to be safer than average.

6. The owning of dividend-paying stocks also has tax benefits. Capital gains trigger a taxable event only when equities, like when common equities are sold. The main tax benefit is that the profits federal maximum income tax rate at present only amounts to 20%. This tax rate is lower than the bond interest rate, which is often taxed at the

same rate as your wages. Usually, 20 percent is far lower than your marginal tax rate for other sources of revenue.

As you can see, stocks paying dividends have properties that distinguish them from the stock market as a whole. These inventories may be part of your investment portfolio.

Why You Should Own Dividend Stocks.

Warning! The dividend stocks must never be ignored.

Most people enter the stock market attracted by great profits news. We all heard of these incredible stories of a rookie's millions in record time. But, of course, we also want to gain money quickly and feel that the stock exchange is the place to make a lot of money. So then we start with a small monetary investment. Then, when it grows, we invest it back, hoping that we will get more money. Finally, many of us generate excellent revenues at last, but this rarely happens fast.

However, there are those who make wrong decisions of all kinds and end up losing even their investment. That is just unfortunate. Perhaps in their investment approach, they should be more conservative when they select stocks in which to invest.

In fact, Plan B is always recommended, at least as a backup. And at any time on the market, we would even suggest that you test at least two techniques. First, although the risk is always lower, always invest some of your money in dividends stocks. Moreover, as a dividend payout, you can keep earning money from them. Second, you can invest in large-scale inventories with the remainder of your money, which can yield a substantial return, but where the danger is also increased.

A dividend is a payment paid by the management to a firm's shareholders. At the end of the year or each quarter, it is paid from the profit. In fact, a dividend is a profit-sharing among investors, all part of the company's owners.

Why It Is a Good Idea to Own Dividend Stocks.

There are three very solid reasons for always keeping you in your portfolio with a few dividend shares.

1. **Dividend stock is risk-free**- Naturally, nothing is entirely risk-free on the stock market, but you can assume that if a firm can pay dividends, it must be very good and confident about the future. These are generally companies with a solid foundation and a fantastic future. And these enterprises are also profitable. So the purchase of these equities makes sense.

2. **You can invest the money back-** some businesses will allow you to reinvest the dividend. In addition, they offer more stocks of the same value rather than paying you the money. Finally, when inventory prices rise, you make more.

3. **Dividends give you passive income**—We all want to do what we love while our investments continue to make

money for us. You might satisfy this wish by investing your money in dividend stocks. Pick just some good stocks with dividends and put your money in them. Then each quarter or year, you can start earning the dividends. You may even improve your dividend profits by using this money. It is certainly appreciated for the monthly payment.

Ways to Find the Best Dividend Stocks.

Dividend investment may be very profitable. When it comes to discovering the best stock of dividends, you undoubtedly want to find suitable candidates to be bought with an automatic stock dividends screener. Screening is a means to search for stocks that fit your specific criteria in the stock market. While many stock screening programs are available, the characteristics of good dividend stocks need to be understood so that your screening tool can assist you in filtering out unacceptable choices.

This would be like advised to use the following qualities to locate great dividend stock applicants to make a simple dividend stock screener for the top dividend stocks:

Dividend yield - The dividend yield may be mainly computed in one manner - by either taking the 12-month dividend trailer or the expected 12-month dividend and then dividing it by the current stock price. Dividend yield may be computed in two ways. First, you prefer to purchase dividend stocks that are more profitable than the general market. Second, stock market yields and stock yields fluctuate over time, with stock prices moving up and down and dividend businesses changing, so checking these elements right before buying a stock is a smart idea, not relying solely on data you have collected earlier. I would propose seeking shares with a dividend yield of at least 4% to 5%.

Profit—also referred to as profits for growth of companies, and above all profit for us, is the payment of dividends in healthy stocks paying dividends (see the following paragraph for further debt payment for some companies by taking on more debt and distributing that amount to shareholders). Although there are various ways to gauge profitability, the return on equity is one common metric featured on most inventory screens (ROE). The higher, the better for ROE. We hope to achieve a minimum ROE of 10% to 12%. Another excellent sign of profitability is the earnings per share (EPS) available on many stock screeners – the higher, the better.

Debt - Many of the best dividend shares are from large, mature, and long-term debt corporations in the process of growing into the current condition. The debt concern is that too much can pose a problem for future payments of dividends if the company is put into a hard patch and earnings fall so much as to require the money it typically pays as dividends to pay off its debt. The debt-to-equity ratio can be easily measured. We'd want to see the company funded more with capital than with debt for our purposes. In that way, our dividend stock screener should limit the debt-to-equity ratio to less than 0.5 and preferably seek out even lower firms.

Market Cap - A helpful approach to filter the size of the business you're looking for is known as the market capitalization of a corporation. The total number of outstanding shares equals the market cap multiplied by the current inventory price. Most analysts use this as a corporate size measure. We want strong, reliable, and generally larger corporations to be safer than smaller companies to invest in our dividend; therefore, we want to choose inventories that amount to $2 trillion for market size.

Valuation- This is how much the market pays for a company's profit stream. We desire a low assessment for this because that usually suggests that the stock price of a corporation has been reduced in relation to its income. The P/E ratio is a widely available metric that can help you evaluate a free dividend stock screener.

Dividend Versus Growth Investments.

It is crucial to discover the difference between various investments and what these investments could accomplish for your portfolio if you want to be a new investment or become a savvier investor. You will first want to comprehend the essentials and resolve any uncertainty you have as queries emerge. Of course, the more knowledge you have of investment, the more knowledgeable your judgments will be.

The contrasts between a dividend and a growth investment are resolved. Finally, the decision is made for a common source of uncertainty for novice and emerging investors.

You may choose to look at mutual funds focusing either on growth or on a dividend plan rather than purchasing individual stocks, but you will first have to comprehend each form of investment's basic elements.

Surplus returns are stated and shared with investors with dividend investments, while the profit excess is dividends. Excess returns are reinvested into the Company in growth models, and the only option to realize profits is by settling the shares or selling them shares.

Every investment has advantages and disadvantages that rely on the investor's specific objectives, financial situation, and investment horizon.

Dividend Investing.

Investment in dividends means purchasing dividend-paying equities. The Company distributes a percentage of profits to its shareholders. In addition to the stock market value increase, this offers investors an opportunity to profit from a stream of revenue.

Some of the advantages of dividend shares are that they tend to outperform growth stocks and offer consistent cash flows at regular intervals. In addition, based on stocks that generally provide dividends, the investment may be less risky because a company's financial healthiness is enough to pay shareholders cash. On the other hand, dividends generally require management to make disciplined capital allocation decisions.

Another potential advantage is that recent changes in tax legislation allow some persons to receive federal income tax-free dividend payments. Thus, unless your revenue exceeds the limit specified, you might be more precious than a dollar you make on taxed wages if you receive a dollar from the dividend.
Investors should look at the payout ratio cautiously and select companies with sufficient stable cash flow and revenue to cover dividend payments adequately.

A successful strategy can entail a concentration on high dividend returns, which lead to huge cash flows, or a high growth rate of dividends that now result in lower than average dividends with expectations of strong firm growth over the next five to ten years.

In general, dividend investment is recommended for investors searching for additional liquidity with a shorter time horizon.

Growth Investing

In contrast to dividend investments in growth stocks, the corporation still has money invested and is not paid out periodically. Instead, all surplus returns produced are replenished in the stock itself. In other words, the expansion only makes profits using sales or redeeming of stocks.

You are banking on future forecasts, the likelihood of corporate growth, and the associated value growth of assets when you invest in growth stocks. While dividend-paying firms manage expenditure, growth firms spend on growth. The management is expected to focus on discovering growth prospects within the firm without focusing on delivering dividends to investors.

A growth investment model is a long-term strategy based on the returns so that someone who does not need so much liquidity is usually better off for a longer timeframe.

Reasons to Be a Dividend Growth Investor.

The stock market was one of the longest-term creators of wealth history, and since the end of the 1800s, it had a compound annual growth rate of approximately 9%.

But like most things in life, it is harder to reap the prospective benefits than to do.

For example, the ordinary retail investor, the world's largest asset manager, has made the market unfortunate. Indeed, the annualized return of the average investor over the last 20 years has been 2.1%, compared with annualized returns of 8.2% and 5.3%, respectively, on equities and bonds.

Although the market saw very strong growth throughout that period, most investors finished drinking water after accounting for inflation.

But there is positive news for those trying to create the stock market power and attain financial independence over time. But there is positive news.

Learn five techniques to help you meet your financial objectives and become a better long-term investor as a dividend growth investor. Investing in dividend growth stocks can bring a stable, growing stream of revenues that will finance your necessities, wishes, and retirement over time by keeping your hand constant and keeping you disciplined.

1) Dividends are a Major Source of Long-term Stock Market Returns.

The first justification for being a dividend growth investor is that dividends have a historic role in the overall return of a portfolio. Today, most investors have heard of a stock market where the underlying aim was to increase share price.

However, dividends accounted for around 42% of the entire revenue of the S&P 500 Index between 1930 and 2017. Moreover, dividends represented far over half of the market's returns at critical times such as the 1970s and 2000s. This might happen if stock values stagnate or decrease for a period, but dividend income remains on the rise.

If you think about it like that, it makes natural sense. If you have a growth stock (i.e., one that doesn't pay a dividend), you can only profit by appreciating stock prices. And the market can, as we all know, be intestinally turbulent.

You indicate that you have purchased Alphabet, which pays no dividend. The company has been growing over several years, and the stock price is rising. If the market falls short, such as during the early 2000s tech bubble or 2008-2009, most or not all capital gains could vanish very quickly.

If you had to sell, may you potentially lose 5 or 10 years in some months of unrealized profit? Well, then, for all your patience, you won nothing, and during that period, you saved nothing. But on the other side, you can get an increased income from your investment through a high-quality dividend growth stock, which can reinvest into more shares, providing an exponentially expanding income stream.

In other words, your dividends are concrete and everlasting profits as a dividend growth investor that can never crash. And if your dividends are reinvested in excellent dividend growth stocks over time, you can still better reinvest at reduced after-crisis prices that lock higher returns even as the market drops.

2) Dividends Growth Stocks Have Outperformed the Stock Market Over Time.

While counterintuitive, companies that consistently pay and expand the companies' dividends have traditionally not performed non-dividend equities, increasing the appeal of being an investment in dividend growth. But to be fair, it's true that this period was mainly inflationary since the beginning of the 1980s. As a result, dividend payment stocks could have become more attractive.

Non-dividend, nevertheless, growth-focused payment inventories can also face several unforeseen obstacles. In some instances, your business models can reach a saturation point earlier than intended, or the technology, consumer preference, or competitive landscape can change considerably. If the stock was valued highly, reflecting the company's higher average potential growth, one of these variables could lead to very bad returns for shareholders. But, more crucially, these companies can uncover profitable growth prospects that move needles.

A company can still generate profits and cash but may have to look wider than the company's main business to keep the profits up. Diversification can be helpful, but it also poses a significant danger because management can make poor decisions in allocating money, for example, making spritz acquisitions for which it can overpay and eventually write down later.

True, a corporation is not immune from these dangers just by paying a dividend. Nevertheless, hundreds of companies have managed for more than twenty years to provide stable or growing dividends and keep their payouts intact through recessions, wars, commodity price shocks, technology upheavals, significant changes in consumption habits, and many more.

These companies have been stable, growing, and cash-rich over time, but management must also be more careful with both the company's financial sheet and the investment growth it chooses to make. After all, you have to be much more selective with what acquisitions or investments you make when paying 50 percent of profits to dividend-oriented investors each year. You can't only toss money since you can put the dividend at risk if you mess up, which might often send out the share price cratering (stock option and vested share grants comprise most executive compensation packages).

Simply expressed, a promise to pay dividends gives management teams greater discipline to invest in their most promising projects with their best return.

3) Dividend Growth Stocks that can Help Ensure a Safe Retirement no Matter.

Maybe the main reason most individuals invest is to assure a good retirement level of living. The dividend stocks of growth can indeed contribute to that objective. Many people know the 4% drawdown rule, for instance, that you should sell 4% of your portfolio to live off during retirement.

This guideline was the brainchild of a study. A 1994 study found that the 60% stock and 40% bond portfolio could sustain a 4% withdrawal for good. In other words, selling 4% of the portfolio every year can help offshore annual asset sales. This makes it very difficult for you to lose money on retirement, simply if you hold an S&P 500 index ETF, then sell 4% of the portfolio every year.

In a 2008 analysis, however, the long-term performance of this portfolio would allow you to boost the yearly portfolio withdrawal to 5 percent while still maintaining its portfolio perpetuity if you stick to S&P 500's 100 most productive dividend shares. Thus, a greater dividend growth portfolio could provide you with superior living standards throughout retirement periods.

One reason is that bond returns continue to be close to historically low, decreasing their current income and diminishing their long-term returns. On the other hand, many high dividends stocks nowadays give higher incomes, increase their income, and over time appreciate their value to safeguard your buying power.

Dividend stocks also have an appeal for retirement since, over time, they have shown decreased volatility. Indeed, the standard difference between equities paying for dividends (blue line) has been almost consistently smaller than that of non-dividend payers (grey line) since 1927.

4) Dividend growth inclusion Investors can help you avoid the most significant cause of market failure.

Human emotion is the only primary opponent of long-term profitability. Thanks to a well-studied psychological phenomenon known as "loss aversion," most investment companies can even match up to the market, even if only they invest in ETFs like Vanguard S&P 500 ETFs at a cheap cost (VOO).

This explains partly why we have, first, market booms and crashes. This also shows that people are only piling up into equities when markets increase, frequently greedy after most profits have already been made.

Then, when the inevitable and good correction of the market, the bear market, or the crash occurs, they panic and sell at lower prices. Human nature puts the market at the most significant risk for attaining your long-term investment targets. It is generally risky and expensive to settle in cash in anticipation of the subsequent market correction. For one thing, the returns on the bull market are usually very concentrated.

More shocking still? He referred to another analysis that concluded that a total return on ZERO during this time of 64 years was netted from the lack of the market's best 7 percent performance months between 1926 and 1990. This shows that you need to get your money working for you for as long as possible. This will help you to genuinely prosper on the market and benefit from the magic of composition. So how can investors help with dividend growth? In short, you need to consider your portfolio as an enterprise with a long-term focus on maximizing long-term cash flow and value.

Just as Nike (NKE) and Coca-Cola (KO) do not attempt, in times of market/interest rate instability, to shut down the global economy through their companies, the same should apply to the portfolio. Think of it like this. By focusing on your long-term revenue and your individual firms' growing dividends, you can relax and remember what matters in the long run: cash flow.

Has Deere (DE) deceived only the income? So what!? An increasing global population is projected to increase the demand for food—consequently, agricultural equipment. So not only will long-lasting investors have no relevance for a short slump in a cyclical industry, but maybe a big chance to acquire a strong dividend company. John Deere, after all, hasn't decreased his dividend over the last 20 years and has increased his payout annually by over 9 percent. In other words, you don't worry about a bad quarter or market meltdown since you are a long-term business owner who mainly focuses on the safety and long-standing growth possibilities of Deere's dividend.

This takes us to another essential truth, which can enable you to enjoy dividend growth investment. Whatever the market does, or what kind of high estimates the sport can currently make, something for a careful investor in dividends growth is always on sale. Through a number of business and interest rate cycles, a time-tested company has proved itself able to reward its patient dividends growth investors, so any correction, market bear, or crash is probably only a chance for one of the best agricultural equipment manufacturers worldwide to pay even better prices and ensure greater returns on your capital investments.

Almost always is a market that unreasonably negates anything – be it energy stocks after the downfall of oil, REITs due to rising long-term interest rates, or stocks after the election. Therefore, if you are concerned that purchasing at record highs will just make you lose, a dividend growth investment can give you a long-term, value-oriented stock that can prevent you from keeping the market going and thus set up yourself to have better returns over time.

5) As part of a dividend growth investor, you can make a return on what stock prices do.

Because so much discourse is being said about markets, economics, interest rates, stock prices, etc., confident investors consider listening to pundits vital and, worse even, contemplate acting on their observations. If you have a long-term, value-oriented view on dividend growth, your wealth and income can rise so much easier over time. Take some advice from Warren Buffet: However, the owners of inventories too often allow their fellow owners to behave irrationally through their capricious and often irrational behavior.

Those who have been able to sit silently for decades, too often when they own a farm or an apartment house, get frenzied when exposed to a flood of inventory quotations. They also transmit an underlying message "Not just sit there and do anything." Liquidity is changed for such investors from the unqualified advantage that a curse should be."

Owning dividend growth stocks helps separate the overall profits from market fluctuations in the long term. Bear in mind your dividends instead of fretting about the price performance of your portfolio each day or year. After all, a significant part of the returns will be accounted for. Although the S&P 500 index might fall above 50% in the financial crisis, we have steadily generated income during this time from the stocks in our Conservative retiree's model Dividend Portfolio in our newsletter. Concentrating on securing a safe, growing flow of dividends will help you smooth out short-term stock price noise and focus on what matters.

CONCLUSION.

A dividend is intended to guide the corporation on how to pay its investors dividends. Studies have shown that investors want to invest in firms that pay dividends to their investors, as the payment of dividends is a sign of excellent health in the company. It also draws possible investments, creates more revenue, and expands the richness of stakeholders. However, this should be noted that a corporation must choose the best technique for its company in terms of its historical financial position, predicted future earnings, and internal demands. The residual technique is best appropriate for companies requiring additional cash. The corporation's priority is to reinvest earnings in the company and pay stakeholders in the form of dividends. A stable strategy could be adopted by a corporation that earns sufficiently low payments to its stakeholders. The company must pay dividends at preset rates to its stakeholders, which is usually minimal. After satisfying business requirements, the hybrid strategy provides its participants with low fixed-rate dividends and extra earnings. This guarantees that the parties concerned receive dividends whatever the company's performance.

As with any other company enterprise, investors should evaluate their stock markets. Money can be put into high-risk, high-return start-up firms or into mature and stable cash distributors. In the former case, there are certain expectations. The wager will be speculative. The corporation can make continuous cash distributions to the shareholders if it is successful, perhaps at a distant moment in the future. Or the shares can be sold to another person who sees the value of the future cash payouts. It is a 'trade,' not a long-term investment, however. There is nothing improper with a "trade" or even a lot of it.

Management Skills for Managers.
1. Time Management for Managers
2. Employee Coaching for Managers
3. Team Building for Managers
4. Self Confidence for Managers
5. Negotiation Skills for Managers
6. Customer Service Skills for Managers
7. Assertiveness for Managers
8. Business Etiquette for Managers
9. Listening Skills for Managers
10 Leadership Skills for Managers
11. Communication Skills for Managers
12. Presentation Skills for Managers
13. Stress Management for Managers
14. Decision Making for Managers
15. Conflict Management for Managers.

Series: Financial Freedom at Any Age.
- Achieving Financial Freedom in your 20's
- Achieving Financial Freedom in your 30's
- Achieving Financial Freedom in your 40's
- Achieving Financial Freedom in your 50's
- Achieving Financial Freedom in your 60's
- Achieving Financial Freedom in your 70's and beyond.
- Achieving Financial Freedom in children
- Achieving Financial Freedom in teenagers
- Achieving Financial Freedom in college students.
- Financial Scams to be Aware of in Retirement.

Series: Personal Finance for You.

- Buying and Selling Crypto for Beginners
- Why Investing in Dividend Stocks Makes Sense.

Series: Wealth 2022.
1. Online Entrepreneurship.
2. Starting Your Own Business
3. Wealth Management
4. Passive Income.
5. 12 Steps to Starting your own business.

Series: Excellent Customer Service
1. Excellent Customer Service in Retail
2. Excellent Customer Service in Fast Food
3. Excellent Customer Service in Full Service Restaurant
4. Excellent Customer Service in Teaching.
5. Excellent Customer Service in a Call Center.

Author Bio

D.K. Hawkins. D.K. enjoys reading personal business books as well as spending time outdoors. More books will come in this collection, so please follow on Amazon for more books.

Thank you for your purchase of this book.

I honestly do appreciate it and appreciate you, my excellent customer.

God Bless You.

D.K. Hawkins.

www.ingramcontent.com/pod-product-compliance
Lightning Source LLC
Chambersburg PA
CBHW070657220526
45466CB00001B/478